Jade Summer
COLORING BOOKS FOR EVERYONE

Thank you for purchasing our coloring book!

We hope you have a fun and relaxing experience when coloring.

Everyone who worked on this book appreciates your support.

COLOR BY NUMBER PATTERNS BY JADE SUMMER

COLOR BY NUMBER PATTERNS BY JADE SUMMER

COLOR BY NUMBER PATTERNS BY JADE SUMMER

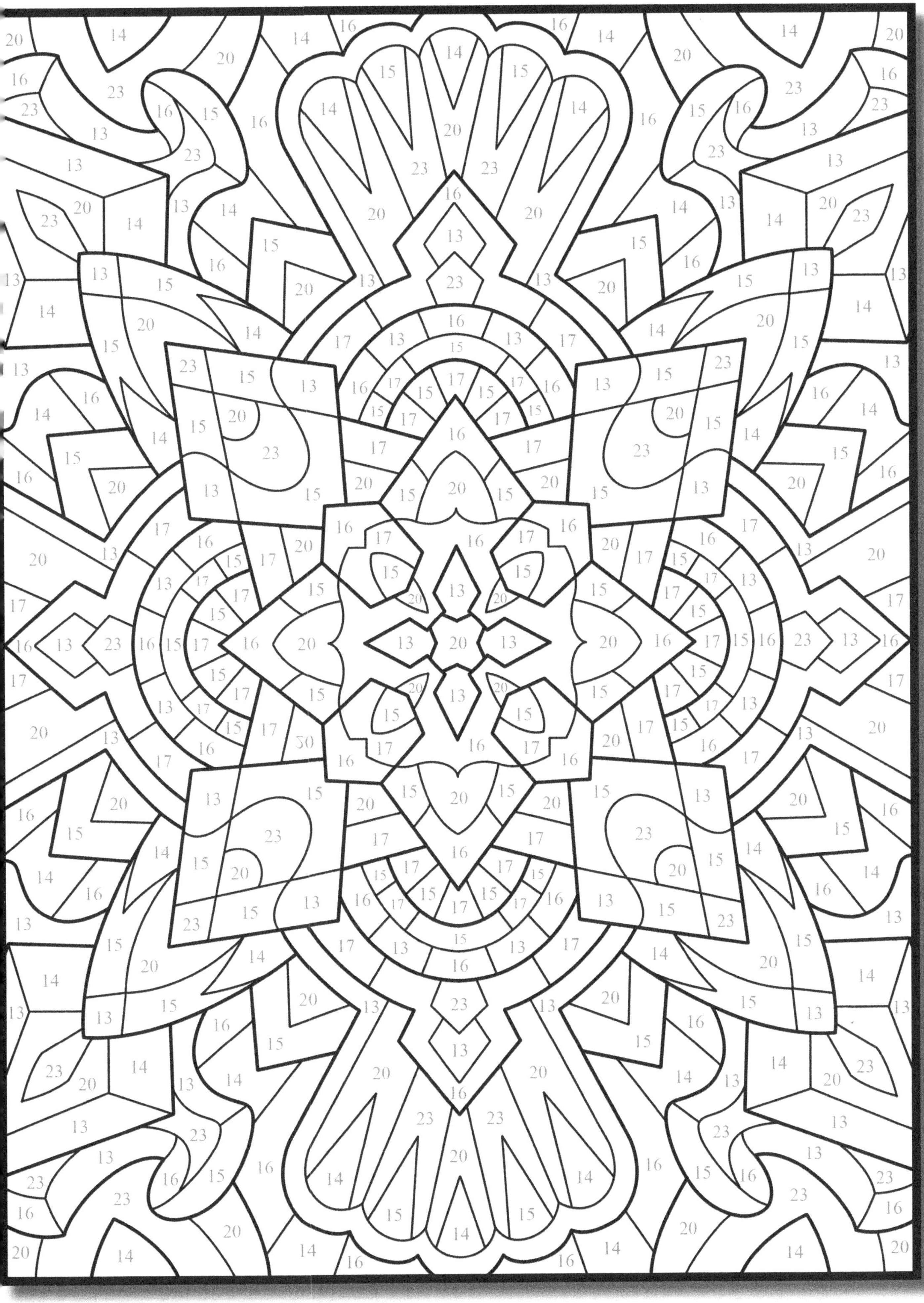

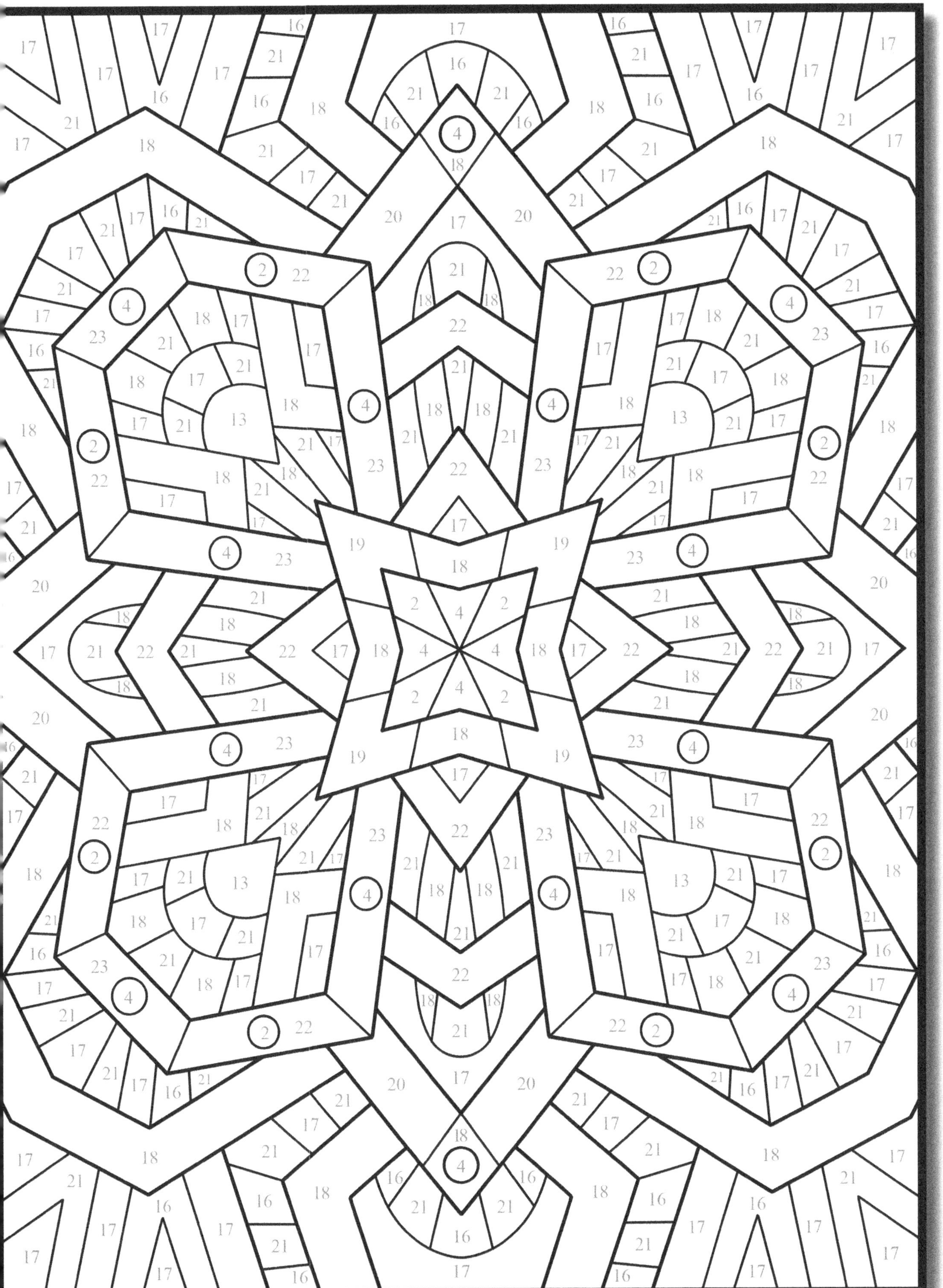

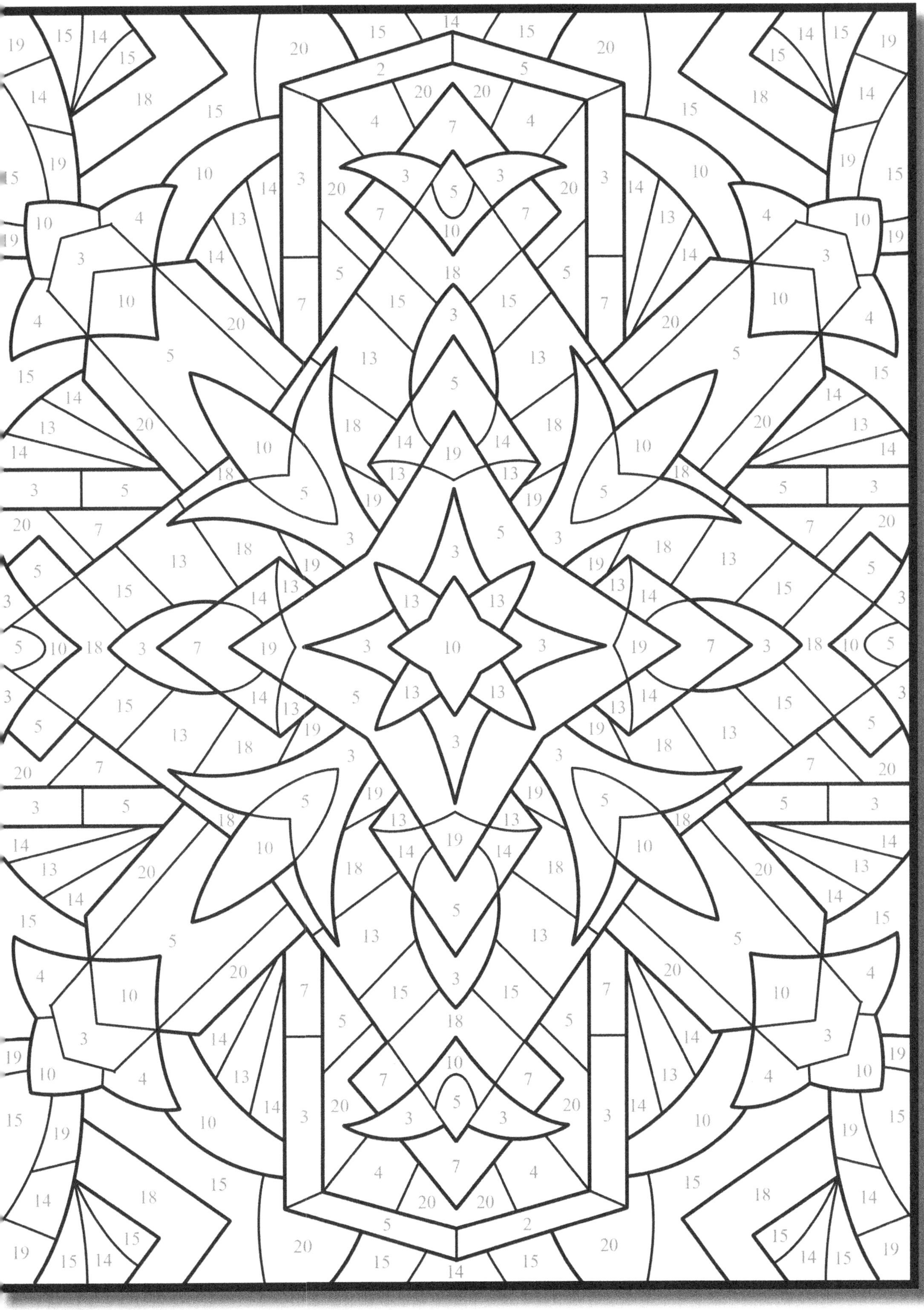

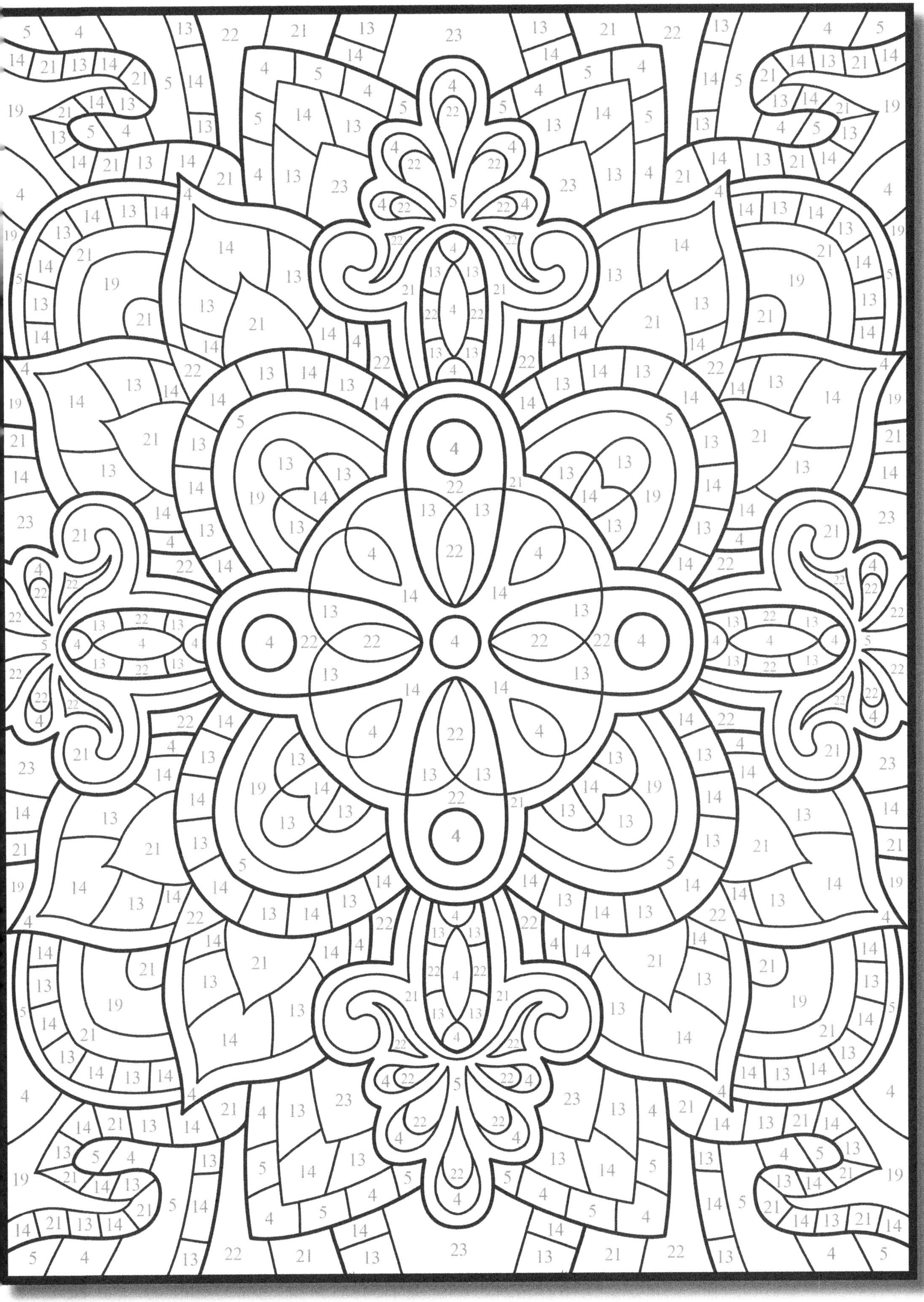

COLOR BY NUMBER PATTERNS BY JADE SUMMER

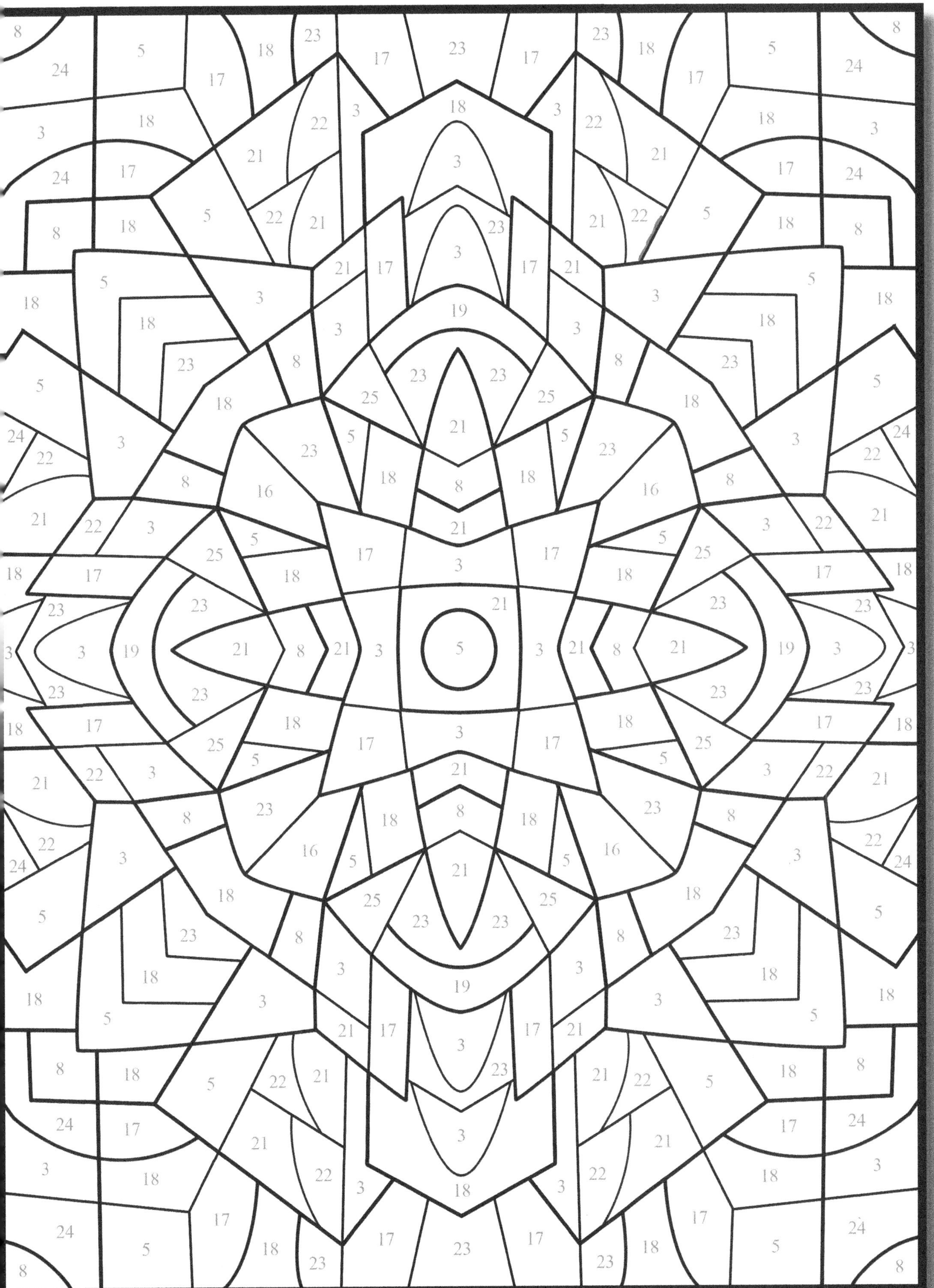

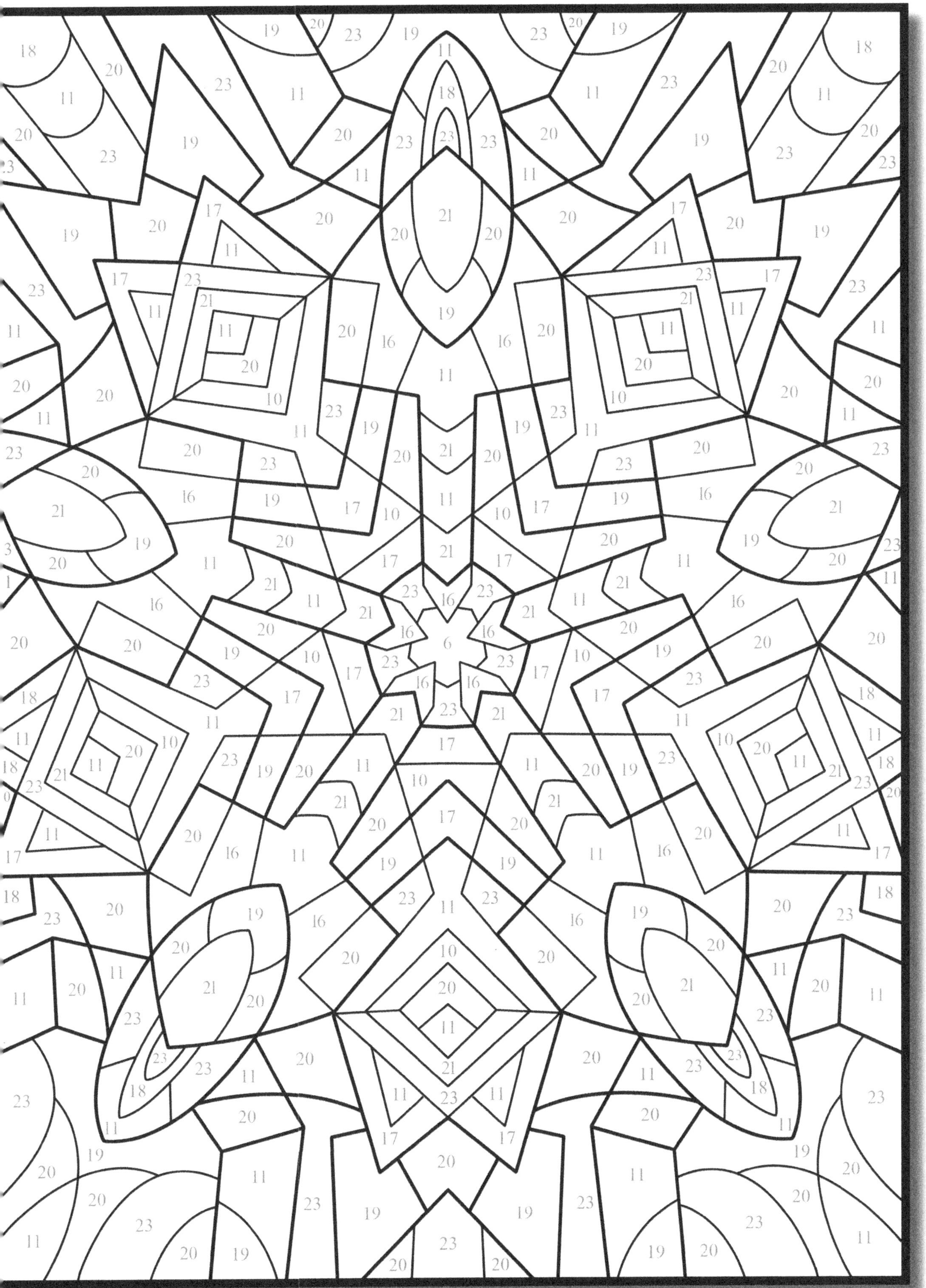

COLOR BY NUMBER PATTERNS BY JADE SUMMER

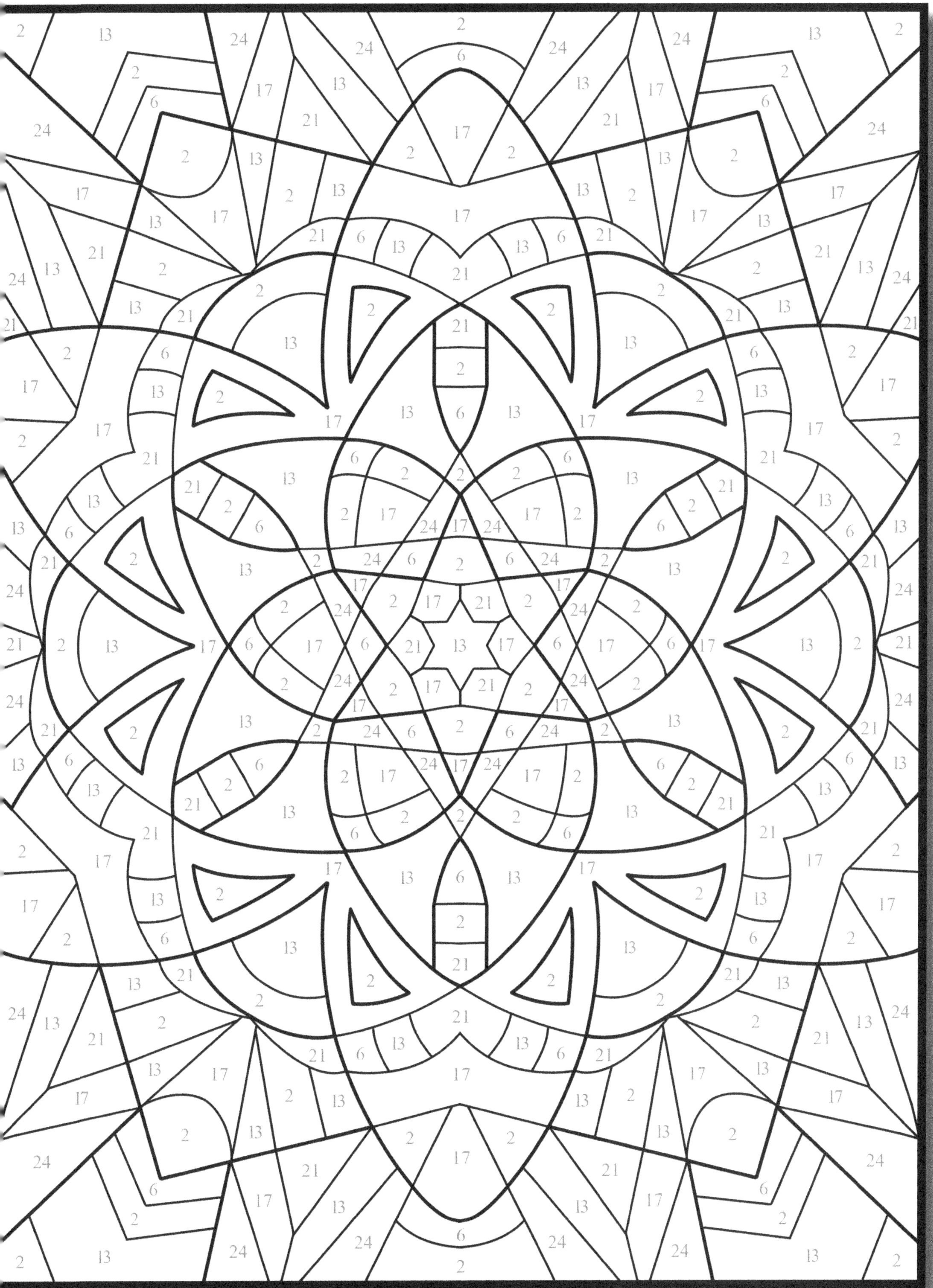

COLOR BY NUMBER PATTERNS BY JADE SUMMER

COLOR BY NUMBER PATTERNS BY JADE SUMMER

CUSTOM COLOR CHART

1. WHITE

2. LIGHT YELLOW

3. MEDIUM YELLOW

4. DARK YELLOW

5. YELLOW ORANGE

6. LIGHT ORANGE

7. MEDIUM ORANGE

8. DARK ORANGE

9. ORANGE RED

10. PINK

11. MEDIUM RED

12. DARK RED

13. LIGHT GREEN

14. MEDIUM GREEN

15. DARK GREEN

16. GREEN BLUE

17. LIGHT BLUE

18. MEDIUM BLUE

19. DARK BLUE

20. BLUE PURPLE

21. LIGHT PURPLE

22. MEDIUM PURPLE

23. DARK PURPLE

24. LIGHT BROWN

25. MEDIUM BROWN

26. DARK BROWN

27. LIGHT GRAY

28. MEDIUM GRAY

29. DARK GRAY

30. BLACK

CUSTOM COLOR CHART

1. _____

2. _____

3. _____

4. _____

5. _____

6. _____

7. _____

8. _____

9. _____

10. _____

11. _____

12. _____

13. _____

14. _____

15. _____

16. _____

17. _____

18. _____

19. _____

20. _____

21. _____

22. _____

23. _____

24. _____

25. _____

26. _____

27. _____

28. _____

29. _____

30. _____

NOTES

This page is for testing and documenting your color choices.

Made in the USA
Las Vegas, NV
06 February 2023

66994487R00063